Life Skills Every 12 Year Old Should Know

Unlock Your Secret Superpowers and
Succeed in All Areas of Life

Hayden Fox

Claim your free gifts!

(My way of saying thank you for your support)

Simply visit **haydenfoxmedia.com** to receive the following:

- 10 Powerful Dinner Conversations To Create Amazing Kids

- 10 Magical Affirmations To Help Kids Become Unstoppable in Life

(you can also scan this QR code)

This book belongs to
to

_____

Table of Contents

Introduction

Hey, kids!

You're getting so big already. There's only one year left until the big One Three. That's right! You're a year away from hitting the teenage years and one step closer to being an adult, complete with adult responsibilities. I bet it's exciting, but probably a little bit scary, too. After all, everything is changing around you. You're hitting a period of physical growth, and your mind is growing and changing, too.

Some things will feel like they get easier as your brain grows, like understanding math or following logic in school. Other things might feel harder, like maintaining good friendships, making good choices, and thinking about what you'll do in the future. Even when things get hard, one of the most important things you can do is make sure that you don't give up. After all, some of the hardest things are the things worth doing the most!

That's why the skills here in this book will walk you through some things that are good to know, and some things that are tough and that will take practice. We'll revisit the Champion Mindset, something I've talked about in other books in this series, and see how you can continue growing your mind. We'll also talk about a lot of skills that will help you to be a good person, like how to stand up for yourself and how to have a serve-first mentality. Other skills will be a bit more practical, like managing money and thinking critically.

These skills may be tough at first, but that's what your support system is for! Your support system is made up of the people you know that you can go to if you ever need anything. They may be your parents and grandparents, teachers, family friends, aunts and uncles, or any other adults in your life that you trust. If you find yourself struggling with anything in this book, or if you have questions or need someone to talk to, those are the people you should go to first.

At your age, it's easy to feel like the adults in your life don't understand you. It's easy to dismiss what they have to say because you think you know better or because things are different now than they were before. However, remember that those adults were your age once. While the world was different when they were your age, they still understand the struggles of being a tween in a world filled with so many challenges and unknowns. Plus, they have the experience in these skills that may be useful to you. Even if you feel like they don't know or they don't understand, they can, at the very least, lend a listening ear to help you feel better.

Before we dive in, try to think of a few adults in your life that you can ask for help from if you need it. Write down their names in a safe space because writing things down will help you remember them better.

Now, let's get started!

Chapter 1: Revisiting the Champion Mindset

Think of someone you look up to in life. Maybe it's a role model you're close to, or it could be an athlete, author, musician, or streamer that you really like. What is it about them that you admire? Is it their success? Often, it's easy to look at other people who are successful and assume that they were *always* good at what they do. You may read a book by your favorite author and tell yourself that there's no way you could ever craft a story as well as they do. Or you could see someone on YouTube with millions of subscribers and think that there's no way you could ever get there.

Want to know a secret?

Once upon a time, those people were your age, too. Once, they were younger than you. At one point, they were a tiny, helpless baby who'd poop in diapers and cry for milk! It can be hard to look at someone that you consider the epitome of success and think of them as such a vulnerable person, entirely reliant on their caregivers for their survival, but I promise you, that streamer you've been watching all year wasn't born with a camera in their face and a mic in their ear! They had to learn and grow, just like you. They had to work hard to get what they have, just like you.

Success comes to those willing to fight for it. It comes to the people who put in the effort. Yes, some people are born with more affinity to certain things than others. Someone might naturally be a strong athlete, but if they don't practice regularly and train themselves, that inner talent isn't enough to make them successful.

Now, think of the opposite. Someone who puts in years and years of hard work, practicing something they truly care about, can still become successful, even if they had to work harder than someone else to get there.

What makes the people you see successful isn't that they're just popular or famous. It's that they had what I call a Champion Mindset. They knew that if they wanted to become a champion, to find success, they'd have to work hard for it, and they did. If you're willing to put in the time and energy to do what you want to do, like those with a champion mindset do, you can make it happen. Your time and energy will pay off, just like it does for them.

A major part of having a champion mindset is to understand that what you do in life isn't fixed. That is, you're capable of learning to do nearly anything if you put your mind to it.

You're capable of learning how to play a sport, how to read music, and how to speak another language, if you're willing to put in the time. You can write a book if you're willing to work hard at it. If you want to be a doctor, you can work toward that, too. Believing that you're capable of learning to do just about anything is known as a growth mindset.

What is a Growth Mindset?

Just like your favorite streamer had to learn how to talk before they could ever stream, you have to grow to reach your goals. Even if you know nothing about what you want to try to learn, you can do it! Even if the first time you try to play the piano, the notes come out weird and you hit the wrong ones, you can still learn with time!

Having a growth mindset means that when you're facing something difficult or when you fail, you believe that you can still learn with effort. It's recognizing that your brain is like a muscle. You can exercise it to help it get stronger, and the same applies with skills. The more you practice something, the better you'll get.

When you have a growth mindset, you get some pretty big benefits. You're able to adapt better because you understand that failing at something doesn't mean that you're terrible or that you're a failure. You know it just means that you'll have to keep trying. You'll be able to get back up again when you struggle because you know that this is all a part of learning. After all, how often do babies fall when learning to walk? If we all gave up every time we failed, do you think you'd see many people walking around and talking? Probably not!

That's because a growth mindset makes you resilient. It makes you willing to dust off your knees and try again from a different angle. You're willing to try something new to reach your goals.

The opposite of a growth mindset is a fixed mindset. This is what you have if you think that one instance of trying something reflects your true abilities. Maybe you try to throw a basketball through a hoop and miss. If you had a fixed mindset, you'd decide that you just can't do this and that you're not cut out for it. You'd insist that you'll never be able to do whatever it is because you can't do it now. Doesn't that sound silly? Do you think that anyone would do *anything* if they gave up after the first few times they failed?

If you're the kind of person who gives up way too easily, there's good news for you. You can learn to have a growth mindset. Yes, that's right – by practicing how to think about things from the perspective that you can learn how to do anything, you can actually make the learning process easier! So, how do you develop a growth mindset? Let's find out!

Developing a Growth Mindset

Accept That It's Okay to Struggle

No one likes struggling, and it'd be great if we could just pick up something new and get it perfectly the first time. However, that's not the way the world works. Nothing in life is perfect, and learning how to keep practicing when things get tough can be difficult. Failure can be frustrating and embarrassing, but it shouldn't be. Besides, if something is easy, then that means everyone can do it, which makes it not have less value. Why is owning a Lamborghini so cool? Because they are difficult to acquire! Always remember that difficulty and value are linked.

Furthermore, failure is a part of life. Struggling breeds creativity. Sometimes, struggling is what brings us to new solutions that we'd never have considered before. Struggling also gives us a chance to continue practicing important skills.

If you struggle with a math problem, for example, you need to practice it more to get it right later. If you're having a hard time scoring a goal in soccer, you'll practice more, and it'll get easier.

Everyone fails sometimes. In fact, look at scientists everywhere. They do so many experiments trying to understand the world, and many of them reveal that what the scientists thought was wrong, and they have to start over. You may have heard of the Scientific Method before – hypotheses (a fancy word for educated guesses) have to be tested, then reworked when they're incorrect. This is a continuous process that must be done until you get the right results.

There's nothing wrong with struggling to get something right. In fact, that struggle is what's going to get you the skill you wanted in the first place, plus appreciate it that much more. Accept it and accept failure as a normal part of learning. It's the only way to get to excellence.

Mindset Affirmations

Affirmations are little phrases that we can use to remind us of something. For example, people with anxiety often use affirmations to help themselves feel better. You can use affirmations that can help you develop a growth mindset, too. The key here is that they have to be effective affirmations. This means that they need to be present-tense, personal, and positive. Then, you need to keep speaking them until you believe them. One of my personal favorites is *I can learn how to do this.* Even if I can't do something now, I believe that I can learn to do it eventually. Other affirmations I like to use include:

- *I'm growing and learning every day.*

- *I'm capable of doing anything I put my mind to.*

- *I know that I can do this if I keep trying.*

- *I can overcome any challenge I face if I keep trying.*

- *My hard work will help me succeed.*

- *I can solve any problem if I put my mind to it.*

- *I will work to achieve my goals.*

- *Everything I value is worth working for.*

- *Every day, I get a little smarter.*

Reflection Time

Sometimes, the best way to help yourself gain perspective is to stop and reflect on your current situation. Have you been struggling with something lately? Have you been feeling like giving up? By learning why you have these feelings, you can sometimes figure out how to get around them. For example, maybe you're frustrated about struggling with your math homework. Instead of letting yourself get so caught up in how frustrating it is, stop and think about *why* you're frustrated. You might be surprised at the answer.

Sure, the homework is frustrating, but there may be something underlying that. For example, maybe your big sibling was in the same math class two years ago with the same teacher and got straight A's while you're solidly in C- territory. It might be less about the homework itself and more about feeling like you're being compared to your sibling that is the problem, and is making you feel like giving up.

Often, other parts of life influence things they're seemingly unrelated to. You could feel self-conscious about something that makes you feel terrified of failure. You could be so desperate to be liked by others that when you struggle with something, you want to give up to avoid embarrassing yourself. But always remember, struggling breeds resilience and strength, and that value and difficulty are intrinsically linked.

Chapter 2: Finding Your Strengths and Weaknesses

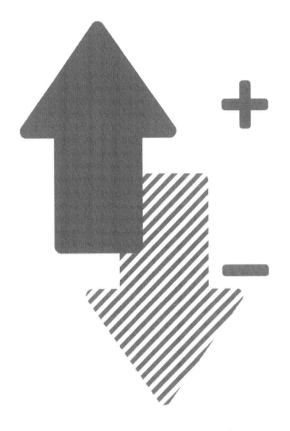

We all have our own strengths and weaknesses in life, and knowing what they are can really help us. You're not limited to pursuing what you're good at, nor do you have to avoid what you struggle with, but it's good to have an idea of your abilities. For example, if you're working on a group project, knowing your skills will help you divide up work because you can each take what you excel at. Maybe you're really artistic while another group member is good with numbers, and another is good at organization. You can divide up the work in such a way that each of you have tasks that play to your skills.

Knowing your strengths and weaknesses can be helpful in nearly every aspect of your life. In fact, this is a skill known as self-awareness, which is an aspect of emotional intelligence. Emotional intelligence is a fancy way of describing your ability to understand and control your own emotions and understand and influence the emotions of others. Self-awareness is one of four pillars of emotional intelligence, which is what helps you to make and maintain good relationships with other people.

You probably already know what an intelligence quotient (IQ) is. It's a number that kind of tells you how smart you are. Well, emotional intelligence is similar to this, but for social skills instead of logic and reasoning abilities.

Knowing your strengths and weaknesses can also help in adulthood when you start trying to figure out what you want to do with your life. Japan has a really interesting word that describes a concept of discovering a passion that brings joy and value to your life. This word is *ikigai*.

The Japanese Concept of *Ikigai*

Ikigai describes a concept where what you love, what the world needs, what you're good at, and what you can make money doing collide. It's a deep-rooted purpose you have in life based on your skills and passions and how you can give back to the world around you.

Maybe you're a skilled artist. You might hear other people tell you that you can't make money as an artist, but that's not true at all. You can create custom art for people. You can work as a designer. You can illustrate books. There are numerous things that you can do with a skill like that, and just because it's not a traditional job doesn't make it any less valuable.

The Benefits of Knowing Your Strengths and Weaknesses

Having a good understanding of your strengths and weaknesses can give you all sorts of great benefits, such as:

- **Better self-awareness:** We already introduced the idea of self-awareness. Another aspect of self-awareness is knowing your abilities and limitations, which you can use to make better decisions from day to day. If you know, for example, that you're not a very good swimmer, you probably wouldn't jump into the deep end of the pool without taking precautions. Likewise, if you know that you're not very good at time management, you may try to set a more organized schedule that's easy for you to follow to help yourself.

- **Better self-esteem:** Self-esteem can be tough, especially at your age. Knowing your strengths and weaknesses can help you to build confidence in yourself because you know what you can do, and you know when it's time to ask for help. For example, if you're not a very patient person, you may ask your friend for a break when a conversation is getting heated because you don't want to get into an argument or say something that you don't mean. This can help you feel more confident in your relationship with the people around you.

- **Better resilience:** When you have a clear understanding of what you can and can't do, you develop resilience and the ability to adapt to situations. This is particularly useful when you're facing a challenge because you'll be able to regulate yourself. That way, you don't get lost in emotions that distract you when you make your decision.

- **Better relationships:** All of this can help you maintain better relationships because when you know your strengths and weaknesses, you can often communicate more easily with others. This is useful when you find yourself in difficult social situations, like facing peer pressure or trying to find a solution to an argument that's beneficial for everyone. The result? A healthier social life!

Learning Your Strengths

Part of learning about your *ikigai* is learning your strengths. This can be hard, but it doesn't have to be. Part of it is understanding that failure is okay, just like we talked about in the last chapter. The other part is exploring lots of different things to find out what you do well.

This means that you need to try new things regularly. You need to be willing to risk failure when attempting to do something you've never done before. You never know – you may not have discovered some of your strengths yet! Explore things that interest you, even if you're uncertain of how well you'll do. If that means that you decide to try playing the ukulele, then give it a solid shot! Don't be afraid to fail or struggle – just try your absolute best.

Once you discover something that seems to come naturally for you that you enjoy, you can start fostering it. Maybe you discover your passion for baking and decorating cakes one day, or you could discover that you're really good at gardening, or maybe you're really good at talking to people and making friends.

Pick up a piece of paper and a pencil and make a list of all the things that you feel you're good at. They could be related to school, hobbies, or anything else. If it's something that you do pretty well and that you're confident doing, write it down. This is a list of your strengths.

Character Strengths

Another part of learning your strengths is recognizing character strengths along with skills. Character strengths like gratitude and optimism are also important to keep in mind. They can help you persevere and pursue your skills along the way.

What's your personality like? Are you perseverant? Do you appreciate the people and things in your life? Do you have confidence and optimism? These are all character strengths that can go a long way in your life.

If you have a hard time identifying your character strengths, try having a chat with your best friend or one of your parents. They may be able to give you some insight into how you're doing and what you're good at. Oftentimes, we don't see ourselves in the same light as our loved ones do, and our loved ones often see a clear picture of us. Your parents might say you're patient or stubborn (which can be a good thing!) or kind.

Add these character strengths to your list of skill strengths.

Learning Your Weaknesses

As tough as it can be to look at personal weaknesses, it's an important skill to have. These are areas in your life where you can take action to improve. You can also use your understanding of your weaknesses to safely navigate situations, like arguments with friends.

A good way to start identifying your own weaknesses is to look at what challenges you the most in life. Are there things that you struggle with that you wish you didn't? Maybe you're not so great at keeping your mood under control, and you get into arguments with your siblings a lot because you say things that you don't mean. That's a pretty big weakness, and it's a pretty big area where you can make improvements.

When you find areas of your life where you struggle, write them down in a journal. Think about why they're difficult for you. If patience is difficult for you, why? Or, if you struggle with doing your homework on time, why? Try to find the answers deep within yourself so you can work around them, or at the very least, be aware of why these are tough areas for you. If you can't find the answer yourself, discuss it with one of your grown-ups and see if you can figure it out together.

And don't forget, even if something is a weakness, you can always work to build upon it with the growth mindset (and likely turn it into a strength!)

Chapter 3: Discovering Your Values

Do you ever get a really strong feeling about something and don't necessarily know why? Maybe you're talking to someone, and you suddenly get a feeling that something isn't quite right when they say something that doesn't make sense. For example, you could be talking to a good friend of yours who you saw at the mall the other day, but she claimed that she was home sick. You know that she lied, but you don't know why it bothered you so much.

The reason it probably bothered you was that what she said and did clashed with your values. If you value honesty in your friends, knowing that your friend was lying to you probably didn't make you feel very good and probably made you start questioning what else she has lied about.

Or, maybe you watched a video online that showed someone bullying a classmate. While the people in the video were laughing, maybe you found yourself feeling uneasy watching it all play out. This can be another example of your values coloring how you feel about a situation. If you value compassion and kindness, for example, seeing someone being a bully could be really upsetting.

Your values guide your thoughts, feelings, and beliefs. In a sense, they are what make you who you are; they make you feel a certain way in certain situations, which lets them influence you. When you feel uncomfortable with a situation, you probably won't participate because it clashes with your values, even if you're not consciously thinking about it. You may just know that you feel uncomfortable with a situation and that's enough to dissuade you.

Does this sound frustrating? It shouldn't! One of the best ways you can be true to yourself is by following and honoring your values. Allow yourself to feel those feelings and let them help you make good choices. Of course, it's still a good idea to have a better understanding of what matters the most to you and why you feel that way. That's where understanding your values comes into play.

What Are Values?

Values are like your roadmap through life. They help you make judgment calls and determine whether certain actions are good or bad. They also help you find your purpose in life.

Someone who's very driven by justice and fairness, for example, may find themselves drawn to being a judge or a lawyer, while someone who values creativity and artistic expression may lean toward being a musician.

Once you discover what your values are, it's like unlocking the key to yourself and understanding who you are. You'll be able to start identifying how these values impact and influence you from day to day. You'll discover how they encourage you and why you do the things that you do.

Some of these values may be influenced by culture or by your parents and the environment that you grew up in. For example, you may learn from your parents that it's important to be kind and to help everyone who needs it, even if it's an inconvenience to you to stop and help. You may have learned the value of honesty and choose to allow that to guide your everyday life. You could be the kind of person who sees loyalty as the most important part of any relationship. All of these are different values that you may hold.

Some really common values that people have are:

- **Determination:** The willingness to keep pushing toward a goal, regardless of roadblocks along the way

- **Tolerance:** The willingness to respect people's differing viewpoints, even when you don't agree with them

- **Generosity:** The willingness to share with other people

- **Kindness:** The willingness to be considerate, generous, and friendly to those around you

- **Honesty:** The willingness to tell the truth

- **Humility:** Having a modest view of your own importance

- **Compassion:** Having sympathy for others and wishing to help them

- **Courage:** The willingness to do the right thing, even if it's frightening

- **Altruism:** The willingness to put other people before yourself without expecting anything in return

- **Empathy:** The ability to understand and share someone else's feelings as if they were your own

- **Self-reliance:** The ability to take care of yourself and your needs

A lot of the reasons we've already discussed describe why values matter. They guide our decisions, which directly reflect our values and personal beliefs. They matter for more reasons than those, though. Another reason that values are important is because they guide us in making social decisions. When adults work together, they often seek out people with similar values because when those values all align with each other, everyone is on the same page. However, when values clash, it gets hard to manage expectations and how people interact with each other.

Thinking About Your Personal Values

All this talk about personal values can be kind of confusing if you've never really thought about them before. After all, it's a pretty scary thing to consider that a few beliefs guide a lot of your actions and decisions! So, how do you find your personal values? It's all about self-reflection.

I'd recommend journaling for this one, as well as thinking deeply about the things that you do that matter to you the most. To help get you started, let's break down personal values into three big categories for now. Adults usually have a fourth category, known as organizational values that aren't so relevant at your age, but will be when you're older.

Individual Values

Individual values are things that guide your own actions and behavior. They can be things like enthusiasm, creativity, or self-reliance. These are important to understand so that you know why you feel the way you do about certain situations.

Need help identifying some of your individual values? Think about three to five things about your personality that you really like about yourself, or a trait that you'd like to have, and write them down.

Relationship Values

Relationship values show how you relate to those around you. They are things that you want to see in people you are close to, like openness, honesty, trust, and loyalty. They help you know the company you want to keep. People who don't have the relationship values that you have often aren't very compatible friends because you find yourself clashing. For example, someone who lies a lot isn't a good friend for someone who needs honesty and trustworthiness.

Think about someone you really trust and respect. Now, write down three to five things about them that have earned your respect. These may give you some clues to your relationship values.

Societal Values

Societal values show how you relate to other people. They can be things like empathy, being environmentally friendly, or wanting to be sustainable. At your age, you're probably starting to understand how you fit into the world around you, and societal values help you navigate that.

Think about how you want to fit into the world around you, then write down three to five ways that you'd be able to do this, like taking care of the planet, being kind to others, or being altruistic.

Chapter 4: Standing Up For Yourself

Have you ever found yourself in a situation where you feel like you're being steamrolled over? Maybe you did something that upset a friend, and now your friend is ignoring you or has decided to tell all their friends about what you did, so they're all bothering you. Or, you could be in a situation where you have a bully picking on you, or you're feeling too shy or self-conscious to speak up about what you really want or need.

Never forget that you matter, too.

Your thoughts and feelings matter just as much as anyone else's, and when you feel like yours are being ignored, or worse, disrespected, you might feel tempted to just suck it up and pretend that you don't care. The problem is this is disrespecting yourself just as much as those other people disrespected you.

One of the kindest things you can do for yourself is to stand up for yourself when you need to. Now, this doesn't mean that you always have to get your way. After all, life is full of compromises, and healthy relationships with friends and family involve give and take. However, you still deserve to have your voice heard just as much as anyone else.

Standing up for yourself can be tough for some people, especially if you're shy, or if you've grown up feeling like it's easier for you to give up what you want to make other people happy. Just remember that when all you do is give up what you want for other people, you're not helping yourself, either. It's one thing to be agreeable or to not care enough about whatever's being talked about, but if you feel like you're being bullied into agreeing to something, it's time to speak up. This can help you build self-confidence and can also help you manage your friendships and relationships better, too.

Saying "No" Can Be Good!

Saying "no" to something doesn't make you a mean person. Sometimes, the best thing you can do when someone wants you to do something that makes you uncomfortable or something you'd rather not do is to tell them "no." For example, if your friend is pressuring you to sneak out of your house at night (which of course, you shouldn't do!), and you feel uncomfortable with it, you should absolutely tell your friend "no." You have to look out for yourself and your peace of mind, after all.

Use Assertive Body Language in Person

Some people make the mistake of thinking that assertive means the same thing as aggressive. You don't have to stand up, shake your fist, and scream at the person you're standing up to. In fact, you shouldn't do that at all since it's likely to escalate the situation. Instead, it's a better idea for you to calmly, but confidently, tell the person you're standing up to that you're not okay with the situation. Make eye contact and stand up tall when you do.

Enforce the Boundaries You've Set

The first time you say no to someone, you're probably going to get a bit of pushback. This is to be expected – after all, they're used to you doing whatever they wanted you to do. The best thing you can do when the other person starts pushing back is to insist that your boundary be respected and ignore the feeling that you need to apologize for standing up for yourself. Any boundaries that you set are valid, even if the other person tried to convince you otherwise, and, in most cases, you really don't owe them an explanation.

Understand When It's Time to Walk Away

Sometimes, even when you try to set a boundary that you want enforced, the other person just refuses to see or respect it. When this happens, you need to know when it's time to walk away from the situation. Now, there will be some situations you can't walk away from, like if you get into an argument with your parents or a teacher at school, but if there's someone around you making you miserable, especially if they're making the environment toxic, walking away can really help. This doesn't mean that you've given in and accepted what the other person had to say. It just means that you need a break, which is a fantastic way to practice self-care.

You Don't Owe an Immediate Response

Especially if you're dealing with someone who's toxic, and it gets to the point that you walk away for a breather, you should remember that you don't really owe people an immediate response – or a response at all. If you have to stand up for yourself against a friend who's pressuring you to do something you don't want to do, it's enough for you to say, "I'm not comfortable with that" and end the interaction.

If you've always felt like you had to do what other people want in life, this might feel unnatural. The people pleasers of the world often struggle with being able to walk away without explaining themselves or apologizing, but the truth is, you don't really need a good reason to not do something a friend or peer is pressuring you to do. There's a chance that you're feeling insecure or feeling like you won't fit in if you don't do what they want, but remember this: Your integrity is always worth more than a few minutes of fitting in with a crowd that wants you to do something that you don't want to do. After all, if they don't care that they're making you uncomfortable, do you really care about what they think? *Should* you care about what they think?

Remember That You Are Worthy of Respect

Even if you don't always feel this way, it's important to know that you are worthy of respect. Why wouldn't you be? Respect is the bare minimum standard of what should be offered to other people. You probably treat random strangers with respect, and they often do the same for you, so why would you think you deserve anything less?

At your age, it's easy to feel dragged into a situation where you feel like the only way that you'll make friends is if you do what everyone else wants you to do, which very quickly can turn into a clear lack of respect for you by the other people who start taking your agreeableness for granted. When you start standing up for yourself, you reclaim that respect that you deserve.

When to Stand Up for Yourself

Of course, not every situation will require you to really stand up for yourself. Sometimes, de-escalating a conflict by walking away is all you really need to do. Other times, you may need to do more. If you're new to standing up for yourself, these are some situations where it's a good idea:

- When someone is insulting, disrespecting, or belittling you

- When someone is trying to discourage you from your passions or hobbies

- When you feel like you can't take on any more work or responsibilities and someone's requesting you do so

- When you find yourself in an unhealthy friendship or relationship

- When you know something is wrong or being done incorrectly

- When you know someone is wasting your time, deliberately or unintentionally

Keeping these kind of examples in mind will help you to start protecting yourself more. They'll help you develop a sense of assertiveness and self-respect that every person should have, regardless of age.

Chapter 5: Advocating for Yourself

As you get older, you may have noticed that your parents are encouraging you to solve more of your problems on your own. This is a good thing! You (probably) won't live with them forever, and, at some point, you need to be able to take care of yourself and your own problems.

After all, who wants to be off at college and ask their mom or dad to email the professor to ask for an extension for them? Not me! And hopefully, not you, either.

Part of growing up is learning to advocate for yourself and your needs. This means that you can tell people what kind of help you need and explain how they can help you. It also means making sure that other people understand your perspective. Advocating is a little different than standing up for yourself. In many cases, when you have to stand up for yourself, you're in a conflict. When you're advocating for yourself, you're seeking a resolution to a problem you have.

Being able to advocate requires you to be able to do a few things. You need to be able to communicate an issue and the solution you want or need clearly and in a way that the other person will understand. You need to have the self-confidence to explain that you have a problem in the first place and the self-awareness to recognize it. You also need to be comfortable with, or at least tolerate, difficult conversations.

During school, you may need to advocate for yourself and your needs to a teacher if, for example, you really need a deadline extension or if you notice that you're struggling and need some help solving the problem. At a job, you may advocate for yourself by explaining that a workload given to you is too high to handle. In a relationship, you may need to advocate for your needs and expectations to keep it healthy.

Self-advocacy gets a whole lot easier to build when you're able to practice it in a safe space, like with your parents. In fact, your parents are a fantastic starting point. Let's say that you want a later bedtime on the weekends because all your friends stay up later and you'd like to be able to chat with them. You may go up to your parents and tell them, "Hey, I really wanted to talk about my weekend bedtime. You know, I'm getting older now, and I want to stay up later on the weekends since I don't have to be up early the next day. If I'm tired or grumpy, it'll be my own fault. I'm so busy during the school week that I don't get a lot of time with my friends, and I'm feeling a little lonely and left out because I know they're up together for another few hours. Can we give this a shot, please?"

When you start expressing your wants and needs to your parents in a way that's more than just saying, "I'm staying up until midnight, and there's nothing you can do about it, ha ha!" you show your parents that you took the time and energy to stop and formulate a well-thought-out reason for what you want, which will be a key in advocating to anyone.

What Should I Advocate For?

In short, you can advocate for just about anything! It doesn't mean that the person you're asking for help from will agree to do what you want, but every opportunity to advocate is an opportunity to practice, and this is a skill that every kid should have.

It's a good idea to advocate for the things that you really want or care about the most, or when you really need help with something. For example, let's say you find yourself in class and realize that you can't keep up with taking notes and following your teacher's PowerPoint. You may go up after class and ask him if he can email you the slideshow. That way, you can review and take notes at home because you're having a hard time paying attention to what he's saying and writing down what's on the slides at the same time.

At your age, your parents may still serve as an intermediary between your education and the teachers that provide it. That's fine, but you're also getting to an age where you can start taking control of the situation yourself. For example, if you get a bad grade on a test, you can advocate for yourself by requesting that you get an extra study session with the teacher to explain what you're struggling with or ask for a way to make up the credit.

How to Advocate

Before you start asking for anything, it's a good idea to plan out what you're struggling with and what you need that will help. Let's look back at that example with the teacher's slideshow for a minute. Now, that speech is something that would come after sitting down to plan what you wanted to say. In this case, you know that you're having a hard time keeping up with the slideshow, and you know that you're missing some information in class, which means that when it comes time to take the test, you'll have some gaps in what you know.

How can you come up with a solution that will help? What would be the biggest support to you at the moment? Sometimes, having multiple solutions can help if it's a particularly complex problem because you'll be able to offer several options that will work for you.

In this case, maybe you come up with three ideas:

1. I borrow notes from someone else in class who's good at taking them.

2. I get the teacher to send me copies of the slideshows so that I don't have to worry about my note-taking in class anymore.

3. I ask him to slow down a bit to give everyone the chance to write down the information on the slideshow before he starts talking.

Well, Option 1 is dependent on a third party, and a teacher might not like that. Option 3 is really disruptive to everyone in class, including everyone who isn't struggling to keep up with note taking. That leaves Option 2 as a potential solution that can be taken to the teacher.

Once you know what your problem is and what you need to solve the problem, you're ready to put it together into a request that you can give.

This sort of planned out strategy can be used for all sorts of conversations, too, from asking permission for something (ask and then give three reasons why the answer should be yes), negotiating a change in responsibilities, to trying to find compromises with friends.

Advocating for Others

While this is a chapter about advocating for yourself, you still have the opportunity to advocate for others as well, but it needs to be done tactfully. Not everyone wants someone to come sweep in and try taking control of the situation. You might see someone struggling and decide to be an advocate for them, but if you don't ask them about what they think first, you're overstepping.

You are, first and foremost, an advocate for yourself. They are an advocate for themselves. If they don't want to ask for help, you can't force the point. It's like the old saying, "You can lead a horse to water, but you can't force it to drink."

If they want you to advocate for them after you ask permission, that's a different story, and you should follow the same strategy you would for advocating for yourself.

Chapter 6: Critical Thinking

When I was in school, I *loathed* the open-ended questions on tests. The ones that had no true right answer, like "What do you think the meaning of the blue curtains was?" or "If you were in the president's shoes, what would you do differently?" were the worst. I could memorize how to spell words and how to solve equations, but when it came down to thinking critically to formulate answers, I hated it.

And yet, critical thinking is so vitally important to our daily lives. The sooner you get comfortable thinking critically, the sooner you'll be able to see the world in a different light.

Critical thinking is our ability to see something with all the evidence and create an informed opinion. This means that we first have to understand what's in front of us, then compare, evaluate, and analyze it. This might sound a lot like making assumptions (more on this later!), but it's not quite the same. In this case, we aren't just following gut feelings and assuming we know the answer. We're forming conclusions that we can support with facts, just like you'd do in science class.

This is one of the most important skills you'll ever learn, because it lets you understand the world around you. It allows you to take in evidence, consider it, and then decide what the most logical answer is.

Learning how to think critically is one of those skills you'll probably be working on for a long while, but it's a really important one. I can't emphasize it enough. When you think critically about the world and events around you, you can often see the truth that's hidden behind assumptions and biases, which helps as you grow up and as your decisions start to become more important.

Critical Thinking and Bloom's Taxonomy

Okay, this is where things might start to get a bit textbook-like, but it's important for you to understand how people use critical thinking. Bloom's Taxonomy is a pyramid that people often use to understand how critical thinking works. It has six layers:

1. Remember

2. Understand

3. Apply

4. Analyze

5. Evaluate

6. Create

As you move from the first layer up to the top, you build upon the skills using critical thinking.

Remembering

The foundation to critical thinking is being able to remember. Of course, this doesn't really require much critical thinking, but it's important as a foundation. This is like memorizing that 5 x 5 = 25.

Understanding

Now that you remember that 5 x 5 = 25, you can start to break that concept down and understand it. This is where critical thinking starts coming into play a little bit more and starts to set you up for application. In this example, it's understanding that 5 x 5 = 25 means that you are adding 5 + 5 + 5 + 5 + 5 to get to 25 because, in multiplication, you are adding the number to itself however many times it's being multiplied by. This is still pretty basic, but once you have a solid understanding of a concept, you can move on to applying it.

Application

Once you get to the application stage, you've mastered a concept in the understanding stage and you can start applying it elsewhere. In math, it means being able to see 13 x 81 and know that in this case, you'd be adding 13 to itself 81 times to reach the solution, even if you don't know what it is off the top of your head (by the way, it's 1,053!).

Analysis

After you've learned how to apply skills, you jump into the real critical thinking skills. When you analyze something, you stop taking things at face value and break them down. You start questioning aspects of what you see and do more research. You may compare and contrast a concept to others or start working on experiments. Analysis is something that's used daily in adulthood, especially in many jobs that require higher education, like being a doctor, lawyer, or engineer. Analysis is where you start casting aside assumptions in pursuit of truth and facts.

Evaluation

The evaluation stage is where you can start combining everything you've done so far and use it to support a decision or opinion. It's where you can defend a choice or determine if it aligns with your values. In adulthood, this is what people do when choosing who or what to vote for and when making important decisions.

Creating

Finally, the last stage of critical thinking is being able to produce new work. It could be an essay written to defend your position or a theory about how something works. It's your ability to take the information and analysis you've gathered and make something brand new out of it.

Let Go of Assumptions

One of the most important ways that you can help yourself think critically is by getting used to questioning and correcting assumptions. You might read something and assume that it means one thing, even though there was nothing in it that actually supports what you said. You might hear that a classmate did something that you thought wasn't particularly smart, and then you may make an assumption about why they did it.

The problem with assumptions is that they don't usually have any evidence backing them up, or if they do have evidence, you could be understanding it incorrectly, which can be a big problem. Instead of making an assumption, choose to learn more. Ask your classmate why they did whatever they did. Do some more research into a topic instead of letting yourself believe what you assumed.

Seek Out Primary Sources

Primary sources are original sources. In journalism, it's when you interview someone who experienced something first-hand. In science, it could be the study that came up with the information that you're using. Primary sources are so important to ensuring that you get the facts right.

If this sounds a little boring, here's an example for you. Let's say you play the game Telephone. If you've never played it before, it's when a group of people stands in a circle and one person whispers something into the ear of the person standing next to them. That person then has to whisper what they heard into the next person's ear, and so on, until it's been whispered to everyone in the circle. What the first person said and what the last person said are probably quite different, because as the phrase was passed around, people misheard it.

The same thing can happen with sources. If you use a tertiary source, something that refers to a secondary source, which refers to a primary source, you may not be getting the information exactly as intended. It's the same concept as why you should never believe rumors, since they have a tendency to get warped over time into something barely recognizable as the truth.

When you want to think critically, the most important thing that you can do is get as much primary data as you can, so you know that it's coming straight from the original source and isn't getting distorted. If you have to use a secondary source, it's important to make sure it's not something biased. For example, let's say that the mayor is being interviewed outside of a brand-new pizzeria and says, "I hate pizza. It's greasy and always spills on my shirt, and I'm sick and tired of replacing my good shirts because they have these big grease splotches on them! But, this pizzeria that just opened up? That's the best pizza I've ever had. It's worth the risk to my shirts!"

His speech is the primary source of information. Now, imagine that the owner of the local newspaper is running for mayor next month during the next election. He hears this speech and sees the perfect opportunity to make people angry at the mayor. He ran a headline the next day saying, "'I Hate Pizza!' Is the Mayor Setting up New Pizzeria to Fail?" with a picture of the mayor scowling underneath it. He doesn't print the whole speech. He just focuses on the negative things that the mayor said to anger the people of the town.

Now, do you think that secondary source is reliable? Does it accurately portray what was actually said? In some cases, especially about politics, news sources can distort the truth to fit their narrative, meaning that they pick and choose what's reported just to make sure that they control how people see the situation. That's why it's so important to investigate primary sources whenever possible. Anyone who looked up the actual interview would know that the newspaper reported the information in the wrong light, manipulating how people understood the situation. Remember, when you're ready to think critically, it means doing research and doing your due diligence to understand the whole picture. Otherwise, you could wind up falling for tricks like the one the newspaper owner used in the example.

Chapter 7: Respecting Yourself and Others

Respect is one of the most important things that we learn through social interactions. To respect someone is to accept them for who they are without judgment and to treat them kindly. It's something that's easily given to other people, but all too often, it's hard to remember to give to ourselves. When you respect other people, you help forge better relationships with them. You create feelings of trust and safety within the relationship, which can help keep it healthy.

However, respect can be taken for granted when it's given to someone who won't give it freely in return. You can also disrespect yourself by not taking care of yourself or making sure that your needs are met. Respect can be tough to build, especially toward yourself, but it'll also improve your overall wellbeing, if you can.

Let's talk about Emma. Emma's a sweet girl, 12 years old. She's quick to help everyone around her and always has a smile on her face. She's eager to please and is careful not to step on anyone's toes as she goes about her day at school. However, when other people make fun of her or try to get her to do their homework for them, she always gives in and doesn't stand up for herself. Instead, she just quietly sits there and apologizes for the inconvenience to whoever was teasing her with a smile on her face.

Emma lacks self-respect. She doesn't believe that she deserves to be respected by others, so she lets them treat her however they want, but she always treats everyone around her with the utmost kindness and respect.

Emma needs a lesson in self-respect, and if you can relate to her, you might need one, too. While it's good that she doesn't let other people get to her when they start saying or doing mean things, it's also not fair that she doesn't respect herself enough to tell them that they're wrong or to set boundaries to be treated with the kindness and respect that she shows to others.

Every single person is deserving of basic respect. It doesn't matter what someone else did or why, they deserve to be treated the way you'd like to be treated just because they're human. Some people call it basic human decency. It's treating people in a way that you'd be okay with.

Some people can find themselves stuck in treating other people the way they have been treated instead of the way they want to be treated. When this happens, you might find yourself in a position where you have to set a boundary to ensure you're treated respectfully. Sometimes, setting boundaries can be a way of helping the other person too because you're communicating with them about how you feel and how you want to be treated. That's a good thing because they might begin applying that to their own lives!

So, in a way, respecting yourself helps you to show respect to others as well.

Why You Need to Respect Yourself

Self-respect impacts just about every aspect of your life. It influences your friends and social relationships. It can control your sense of self-esteem and self-worth. Healthy self-respect can make you feel happier because you're not relying on other people to make you feel good. You're making yourself feel good, instead.

Self-respect is also important in committing to your personal values. When you have self-respect, you're more likely to stand up for those values and set boundaries to protect them. People with a healthy self-respect are willing to uphold those values because they wholeheartedly believe in them. This can help them develop a sense of self and dignity, knowing that they'll honor their deepest beliefs.

Without a strong sense of self-respect, it's easy to feel like your only sense of worth is what other people assign to you. For example, you might rely on other people for validation, meaning that your value is tied to how happy you make the people around you. This can be a lot of pressure over time, as you continually forego what you really need to help other people, instead. As a result, you may feel like your life doesn't have much meaning. When you forego self-respect and sacrifice your most important values, you may feel guilty and anxious.

This can all come together to leave behind unhealthy relationships. If you don't see your own self-worth and don't have self-respect to defend your boundaries, you may find yourself in a position where you allow people to take advantage of you. You could have friends that know that you'll do whatever they ask, so they push those boundaries as far as they can, leaving you feeling uncomfortable but afraid to say no.

None of this is any good for you. Maybe you've heard the saying "you can't pour from an empty cup." This is exactly what that phrase describes. When you spend all your time taking care of other people and making sure that they are happy instead of worrying about yourself, you can put yourself in a position where you empty your cup, so to speak. In other words, you make it so that you've given so much of yourself to everyone else that you don't have the energy to take care of your own needs.

How to Practice Self-Respect

Practicing self-respect is all about recognizing that you have to take care of and love yourself just as you do others. This means knowing when you can say no, knowing when to set boundaries, and knowing how to defend them. If you're spending so much time trying to please everyone else, how do you please yourself? It's not enough to help other people. You need time to enjoy yourself. You need to be able to engage in self-care, meaning that you do the things that you need, like exercising, spending time on hobbies, and resting when you need it.

To start practicing self-respect, you need to make a commitment to yourself to put yourself first. This doesn't make you selfish or a bad friend or person. It means that you care about yourself. Take a personal day. If you need time to yourself, don't be afraid to tell a friend that you can't hang out that day. Turn down invitations to do things that you don't want to do.

Another major part of self-respect is accepting and loving yourself, which can be tough for people-pleasers. One thing that you should remember is that you are perfectly you, and that's enough. You don't have to be perfect. You don't have to be a perfect friend or perfect child to your parents. You don't have to be a perfect student, either. You just have to be the best possible version of yourself.

Improving Low Self-Respect

If you struggle with self-respect, you're not alone. A lot of people do, especially if they've spent their whole lives worrying about other people. However, if you want to improve how you treat yourself, there are some easy ways you can do so:

- **Honor Your Values:** We've already talked a whole lot about values because they're so important. Being able to honor your values means acting in ways that align with them. This means that you don't let people pressure you into doing things that go against your values and setting boundaries that protect them.

- **Focus on Internal Qualities Over External:** How much value do you assign yourself based on external qualities? A lot of people fall into the trap of thinking that they're only worth as much money as they have, or how beautiful they look or the number of followers they get on social media. There's a big problem with all of these, and it's that they focus on external values. These have nothing to do with who you are as a person, and rather reflect how other people see you. When you focus on image instead of who you are as a person, you're not able to live an authentic life being true to yourself. Don't concern yourself with how other people see you. Worry about who you are as a person, instead. Your character, values, and actions are what ultimately define you as a person.

- **Accept Who You Are:** Do you often have bad thoughts about yourself? Maybe you tell yourself that you're not good enough or that you're dumb because you didn't get a perfect grade or because you got into an argument with someone, or you might think that because you didn't get first place at something, you're a failure. Here's the problem with this thinking: You're defining yourself with actions. It's okay to feel frustrated or upset when something doesn't go according to plan, but the last thing you should be doing is calling yourself names over it. Instead, you should be focused more on accepting yourself. Stop being your own worst critic and instead accept everything about yourself. Your flaws, struggles, and other things you don't like about yourself aren't what define you. Forgive yourself for being just as imperfect as the rest of us and remind yourself that failure is nothing more than an opportunity to keep learning. In fact, when you fail at something, you learn something: what *didn't* work. And that's worth celebrating!

- **See Your Negative Thoughts and Challenge Them:** A lot of our own inner criticisms come from negative thinking about ourselves. You might say that you're stupid because you got a C on one paper two years ago, even if you've gotten nothing but A's since. This right here is a negative thought. You're letting yourself be distracted by the one time that things didn't go according to plan and letting that define the entire situation. When you catch yourself doing this, the best thing that you can do is to stop and challenge the negative thought. For example, maybe you aren't particularly good at painting, but you love it. Instead of criticizing yourself for not painting a masterpiece, tell yourself that you don't have to be perfect. You still deserve respect, and you enjoy what you're doing.

- **Remember That Self-Doubt Lies:** Finally, when you find yourself questioning whether you can do something or whether you're worthy of being treated well or loved, remind yourself that your self-doubt is lying to you. If you have that little voice telling you that you don't deserve to be treated kindly by your friends because of who you are, remind yourself that it isn't true and that everyone is deserving of respect.

By using these tools and starting to change how you think about yourself, you can start respecting yourself more. All it takes is a little willingness to change your mind and improve your view of yourself.

Chapter 8: Learning Money Management for Tweens

In my experience, there are two types of people when it comes to money management: those who save and are responsible with their money and those who spend it faster than they can put it in their wallets. Which one are you?

Here's another question for you. A magic genie pops up and offers you two choices: You can have one penny today, but it's a magic penny that will double every day for 30 days. Or, you can choose to have $10,000 cash each day for 30 days. Which one would you choose?

We'll talk about the answer to the second question in a little bit. Think about it and write down the reason you chose what you did. In the meantime, it's time to start talking about money. Yeah, yeah, money isn't exactly a fun life skill, but it's one that every person needs. You might think that the ultra-rich don't bother saving, investing, or budgeting, but how do you think they got their wealth to begin with? The people who stay rich are the ones who learn the proper money skills. That's how they make their wealth, then continue to make it grow.

Differentiating Between Needs and Wants

Before we begin, it's important to start thinking about the difference between a need and a want. Yes, this is something you're already pretty familiar with, but is it something you put into practice? You might feel like you really need that new pair of shoes or that game that just came out, but do you? Will you die without it? You might feel like it when you see your friends playing the game or you're at school in your old pair of shoes, but in reality, no. You'll be just fine.

Needs are things that you can't avoid spending money on. Things like food, a home, power, and water are all necessities. They're the things you need to take care of yourself and live your life.

Wants are nice to have, but they aren't absolutely necessary. For example, that new pair of shoes may not be a need if you already have shoes that are in good shape. But if your current pair is too tight or has a hole, it may actually be a need.

Right now, your parents are probably paying for most or all of your needs on their own. That means that you might feel like you can spend the money that you get however you want. Technically, that's between you and your parents, but spending every cent as you get it isn't smart. It's okay to treat yourself every now and then within reason, but don't feel like you have to waste all of your money on every single want that crosses your mind.

Start Saving Early

That brings us to our next point: savings. It's easier to get into the habit of saving money while you're young and have money that you can play with than when you're an adult working your first job and paying bills on your own for the first time. When you start saving now, you set the habit that's easy to stick to once you go off into the world on your own.

Think of this as financially brushing your teeth. When you were a toddler, you probably *hated* having your teeth brushed. Now, you probably do it twice a day out of habit without even thinking about it. That's because it's a habit that you've developed, and it's one that comes automatically.

By making saving an automatic habit, you'll start pushing money into a savings account for future needs or for major financial goals you may have. You might not be thinking about going to college or buying a car or house right now, but in a few short years, these will all be on your mind. I promise you, adult you will thank you if you set this habit now when you've got a comfortable savings in the future.

Set a Budget and Pay Yourself First

How much you save will be dependent on a budget and how much money you have. Maybe you walk your neighbor's dog twice a day in the summer while you're out of school and your neighbor is at work, and he pays you $20 a week for your time. You might want to throw that $20 toward something like currency in a video game, a book, or a ticket to the movie theater every time you get it, but doing this isn't helping you in the long run.

I love the "pay yourself first" method, which means as soon as you get paid or get money, you pay your future self by putting a portion of it away. If you're getting $20 per week, saving a portion of that might seem kind of silly at first – after all, it's probably just a few dollars, right? Well, this is a great way for you to build a habit, even if the money in your savings doesn't grow as quickly as it would if you had more.

To figure out how much money you can save, you need to figure out what else you're spending money on. Now, as a 12-year-old, you probably don't really have any expenses to worry about, other than paying for any extras you may want. As a general rule for adults, you should save at least 20% of your money when you get it. This is a great way for you to start socking money away for a rainy day, or to buy that new game console you've been eyeing.

If you do have things that you spend money on regularly, you can put it all into a budget to help yourself see where it all goes. For example, maybe you spend $10 per week on Robux, $5 per week on a treat when your mom goes to the coffee shop on Saturdays, and $5 goes straight into savings. Your budget is really straightforward. You know that if you spend any money on something else, it has to come out of one of these categories because you've already spent it.

Budgeting becomes more of a factor when you start adding on bills and recurring payments, like for a Netflix subscription or a phone bill. However, it's important to have an idea of what a budget looks like. You might also consider asking your parents about their budget and seeing if they'd walk you through how they manage their finances so you can see a full household budget in action. It might surprise you to see where all the money goes!

Shop Smart

Another way to be money savvy is to understand how to shop well. This means using coupons, paying attention to weekly ads, and otherwise looking for discounts. After all, if there's a discount available and you choose not to use it, you're wasting your money that could have gone to other things! This doesn't mean that you need to start clipping every coupon you see, but if you notice that something you want is on sale, it might be a good time to buy it if you've got the cash saved up.

Another way to shop smarter is to take a look at what something costs at different stores. Nowadays, with the internet, it's easier than ever to shop around and make sure that you get the best price possible.

Compound Interest and the Magic Penny

Now, let's go back to that magic penny for a minute. Did you choose to take it, or did you opt for $10,000 per day? If you chose the $10,000 daily, you chose the wrong option! Here's why. When you double a penny every day for 30 days, it grows REALLY quickly. On Day 1, it's only worth $0.01. On Day 2, it's just $0.02. By Day 15, it's $163.84. I know, you're sitting there thinking I'm crazy for saying the penny's the right choice now! After all, by Day 15, you would have had $150,000 had you chosen the $10,000 per day!

Here's the catch. Day 16 increases to $327.68. By Day 20, it's $5,242.88. This is where the numbers start shooting up. By Day 25, the value of the penny is now $167,772.16. By Day 28, it's $1,342,177.28. That's right, over $1 million. And on Day 30? It's worth a massive $5,368,709.12. Had you taken the $10,000, you'd only have $300,000 by the end. Yes, it took until Day 26 for the penny to be worth more than the $10,000, but it's worth a lot more money in the end, right?

That right there is the power of compound interest, and it's exactly why the sooner you save, the more money you'll have if you stick it into a savings account with a decent interest rate.

Interest is the value of your money growing with time when it's kept in certain accounts or investments (don't worry we will discuss this in further detail in future books). Compound interest puts the interest that you earned back into your overall balance, allowing the interest to earn interest as you grow it.

It's a slow ride when you use compound interest to invest your money, but as you can see, the more time the money has to grow, the larger the value will grow with each passing year. In fact, compound interest is so powerfull that Einstein labelled it as the 8th wonder of the world!

Chapter 9: Planning Your Future

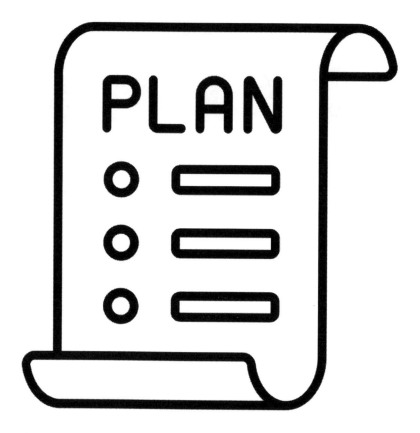

At 12, your future probably feels so far away. After all, you've got six more years until adulthood – that's half of your life right this minute! That can seem like a long, long time. The thing is though, time flies. As you're growing up, you're going to start facing pressure from adults to figure out what you want to do when you're out of high school. That's a lot to put on the plate of a middle schooler! However, you can break down planning for your future and start thinking about what you want to do and how you can achieve your goals now.

When I was your age, I didn't know what I wanted to be. I had a friend who was dead set on becoming a model. I had another friend who wanted to be a rock star and another who wanted to be a doctor. Of the three of my friends, the first two never really took anything seriously. After all, they'd tell me, how much do their grades really matter if all they're going to do is to become a model or to rely on their voice? My friend who wanted to become a doctor was, ultimately, the only one of the three who ever actually achieved her middle school dreams. The last I knew, she was busy working as a pediatrician, happy as a clam and living her best life.

So, what was the difference between the three? It wasn't *what* they wanted to be that made the big difference. After all, there's nothing wrong with being a model or a rock star. The world needs beauty, and it needs good music. The problem was, they didn't plan for it. They didn't put in the effort to bring their dreams to life, and because they were convinced that school wouldn't matter, they weren't doing so hot once it was time to apply for college.

My doctor friend, though, took everything seriously. She was already studying for the SATs in middle school! It blew my mind – I didn't even know the test existed at that age, and yet, she was already diligently studying for it. Ultimately, her drive and her rock-solid plan brought her the success that she so desperately dreamed of achieving, and I couldn't be happier for her.

You can do the same thing, as long as you're willing to get started. If you think college is in your future, now's the time to start thinking about your grades and making sure that they're as high as possible. Now's the time to start finding ways to make you look competitive by participating in extracurricular activities and volunteering, if you can.

This might all sound really overwhelming, but it doesn't have to be. Let's dive into some future planning.

Ask Yourself Questions

The first step to planning your future, of course, is to determine what you want to do in the first place. Here's the thing – anything can be a viable plan for the future if it's well thought out. At your age, you might not be 100% sure what you want, and that's fine! However, it's a good idea to start considering whether you plan to go to college or to get a job right out of high school.

Even if you're not totally sure what you'll do once you graduate from high school, having a general plan is better than just running in blindly. If you *do* want to go to college, having a solid plan is one of the most effective ways to make your dream a reality. If you decide right now that you don't know if you want to go to college and then don't plan accordingly, you could find yourself realizing that you're at a big disadvantage when application time rolls around if you weren't prepared in advance.

Try writing out answers to these questions to help you start piecing together what you want to do with your future.

- If money was no object, what would you want to spend the rest of your life doing?

- Do you enjoy school and studying? Is it something you'd be willing to commit an additional four years to?

- What subjects do you enjoy? What careers align themselves with those subjects?

- Do you want to stay close to home or move far away?

- What kinds of careers do you *not* want to do?

All of these questions can provide you little details about you and your preferences that might help you. If you said that you want to be a software programmer in response to that first question, for example, then maybe that's something you should consider going to school for. On the other hand, if you said you'd run a pet rescue, you might want to consider a veterinarian program. Either way, exploring your interests now can reveal what you may want to consider studying in the future. If you think you'd enjoy a job that would require a college education, you can start planning for it. Alternatively, you may realize that what you want to do with your life will take you down a different path, like an apprenticeship or trade school.

Entrepreneurship is another fantastic route to go down if having your own business interests you. Although it can be very rewarding, it can also be just as difficult (but remember that value and difficulty are intrinsically linked!). What makes entrepreneurship so great in this day and age is the fact that the internet makes it accessible for anyone to start an online business. If making money from your computer interests you, search "online business ideas" or "online job ideas" on Google and YouTube to get started.

Thinking about jobs or careers that you'd never in a million years decide to do can help you get some information, too, because these will automatically be placed on the chopping block.

If, after answering these questions, you're still unsure, just know that there's no one right way to have a career. College, trade schools, and apprenticeships, deciding to start your own business, or choosing a job that doesn't really require any specialized training are all valid options if you're willing to pursue them and set out a plan that helps you get to that place that you're looking for.

Planning for College

If you've decided that you're definitely going to college for something, or that you might want to go to college but don't know for sure yet, the safest bet is to start planning right away. Middle school is like high school-lite. It's a chance to get used to multiple classes across a campus, different teachers, tests, and harder work before the grades really start to count. Most colleges don't care about your middle school grades – they want your high school transcript, so planning now is a great way to get into good studying habits before your grades will matter much more.

Another major consideration if you want to go to college or think you might go is that many look at what you've done with yourself outside of school, too. They'll look at sports, extracurriculars, and volunteering that you've done over the years because they're not just looking for students with academic prowess; they want to see well-rounded people who can thrive in numerous settings.

Among all these considerations, you'll also probably have to take college admission exams. While these are being required less and less since the COVID-19 pandemic, many schools still require or recommend that test scores from the SAT or ACT be submitted. These are long standardized tests that you take that judge how much information you've retained in school. A lot of times, a high SAT or ACT score can offset a not as high grade point average (GPA), so if your grades are just average compared to your peers or are a little on the lower side for a school that you think you'd like to go to, having high test scores can make a major difference.

Planning to Work

If you're planning on immediately jumping into working after high school, you might have an idea of what you want to do, or you might not. Maybe you've decided that what you want to do is get into a trade, which means you'll need to complete an apprenticeship, or you might decide that you don't care what kind of job you'll work, but you're not interested in studying once you graduate. That's entirely your choice!

No matter what your choice is, though, it's a good idea to at the very least feel out what kind of career you think you want.

Talking to Other Adults for a New Perspective

If you're somewhere in the middle and don't know what you want to do with your future, one of the best solutions is to talk to adults about their choices and experiences. This can help provide insight into what life is like for them and whether they regretted their decisions. Now's a great time for you to start questioning people in different professions that you think you might like without feeling the pressure to choose something right away.

Chapter 10: Finding Your People

Making friends is *hard*. It might seem easy at first, but it takes time to get to know people and find out if you're really truly good for each other. Making friendships can come easily to some people and be hard for others, so if you find yourself struggling to find the right group of people to spend your time with as you get older, know that you're not alone by any means.

In elementary school, a lot of what determined friendships was really just being in the same space as other children your age. You might have had friend groups that you played with at school and others in your neighborhood and others in extracurricular groups. As you get older, you start developing more individualized interests. You might be really into art while someone you were friends with before found their passion in athletics.

While there's no rule that you and your friends have to like the same things, it can really help, especially as you start making new friends in middle school, where oftentimes, several elementary schools come together, meaning you have more classmates.

Friendships are more important now than ever, as you're reaching an age where you'll start pulling away from your parents and becoming more independent in life. Having good friends creates a good support system that can help you when things get tough or when you feel like no one understands you or what you like.

The problem is, people are changing at this age. Someone you were friends with two years ago may now be someone who makes you uncomfortable with their choices. That's why it's so important for you to be able to find your group of friends that aligns with your values and interests.

Quality of Friends is Always More Important Than Quantity

If your first thought when thinking about friendships was popularity, think again. You don't have to be in the popular crowd if they aren't the kind of people that make you comfortable. You shouldn't have to change your interests or do things that make you feel uncomfortable just to be liked by your friends. After all, your friends should care enough about your comfort to not pressure you. If your friends are pressuring you to try things that you don't want to, it's a good sign that your friends aren't all that good for you.

Explore your interests and be yourself. Anyone who doesn't want to be friends with you because you've been your authentic self isn't worth your time. Be who you are. Embrace and love yourself enough to see that some people just aren't good friend material, and that's okay.

Be Friendly to Everyone

The easiest way to make friends is to be friendly to everyone, no matter who they are. Don't get involved in cliques that like to exclude or make fun of people because it's only a matter of time until you're the one with the target on your back being made fun of. Say hello to classmates. Hold open doors if someone needs help, and don't be afraid to pick up a conversation with the person sitting next to you in class if you don't know them.

By being friendly, you make yourself a more approachable person, which also means that you might meet people who have similar interests to you. Whether you're into sports, anime, art, music, or anything else, there are bound to be other students in your class that share your interests.

Part of being friendly is smiling at people, and the other person is likely to smile back at you. It's contagious! This is a great way to break the ice and get to know new people.

Try to Join Clubs Catered to Your Interests

If you're still trying to find your friend group, a great starting point is to join extracurricular activities, especially those that you're truly interested in. When you do this, you're more likely to meet people with shared interests, and the time in your clubs can really help you connect to those around you. Extracurriculars could be sports, art groups, or special interest groups.

If there aren't any clubs that cater to what you like already at your school, you could always consider creating your own. There's a good chance that other people would be interested in joining. Talk to a teacher or school counselor about what you'd have to do, and they may be able to facilitate getting the ball rolling. Clubs can also be out of school, too. You might be able to find one at the local library or community center, which can further expand your friend circle.

Finding Friends When You're Shy

When you're shy, it can be tough to try any of the tips listed previously. I get it! It's hard breaking out of your shell, especially if you don't currently have any close friends. You might be afraid to approach new people, or you could be a new student in the middle of the school year and feel like you don't belong.

It's easy to say, "Just stop being shy." It's a whole lot harder to actually implement it. If you're shy, you might be insecure about yourself or afraid that other people will reject you. This is completely understandable! However, if you're too afraid to approach other people, you may have a hard time finding friendships. Sometimes, you have to take a leap of faith and open up to someone to start finding the group where you belong.

If you're afraid of rejection, ask yourself why. Consider the reasons you're so worried about people disliking you for being yourself. Often, it's all in your head and coming from a place of insecurity rather than being rooted in reality. Lots of people are happy to talk to new people and make new friends.

Something to remember is that if you're worried about being judged and rejected, most of the time, your fears aren't even on other people's radar. Many people are so caught up in worrying about their own image that they're not paying nearly as much attention to yours. They're also not going to shun you just for making a mistake. Most people are reasonable. If you stumble on something, apologize, or maybe make a joke about it, and move on. You'd be surprised how gracious a lot of people are. After all, we all mess up sometimes!

The Importance of Walking Away From Toxic Friendships

A hard part about making and maintaining friendships is knowing when to walk away. As much as it's good to believe that everyone has good inside of them, some people just aren't healthy to be around or to maintain friendships with. This is especially true during the tween and teen years when puberty is occurring and people are trying to forge their own mature identities, but keeping a bad friendship around isn't good for you. It can be bad for your mental health and can also lead to isolation from other people that may be better for you.

Unhealthy friendships might not seem unhealthy when you're in them because they're not bad all the time. After all, if they were, the toxic friend wouldn't have anyone around them. Unfortunately, this can also make it harder to walk away from them when you should. Keep an eye out for these signs that a friendship may not be as good for you as you thought:

Too Much Drama

Let's be honest here. Tweens and teens live in a lot of drama. It's just a part of growing up. However, if your friendship is getting to the point where it's nothing but drama, and it's stressing you out, you may need to take a step back to get some clarity.

Your Friend Tries to Control You

You are your own person, and your friend shouldn't be trying to change who you are or what you do. You are allowed to have your own likes and multiple friendships. You're allowed to spend time with other people. If your friend constantly gets jealous or even angry when you do something with another friend, or if they try to tell you not to hang out with certain people, they're showing signs of being controlling. This isn't good for you or for them. Your friend should be supportive of you and what you do, not try to control you.

Your Friend Gets Mad a Lot

We all get mad sometimes, but if you notice that your friend is mad at you more often than not, suddenly lashes out at you, or gives you the silent treatment, it's a sign that there's something wrong. Healthy friendships require good trust and communication between each other, and that doesn't involve being mad and lashing out.

Your Friend Pressures You

Similar to controlling you, pressuring you into doing things that you don't want to do isn't okay in any relationship. Your friends should support and accept your values and boundaries, especially if that boundary is about not doing something that will get you in trouble.

Your Friend Is Mean

If you've noticed that your friend is mean to you, it's a pretty good sign that the friendship is in trouble. It's one thing to joke around with each other, but a healthy friend won't call you names, insult you, or make fun of you. They should be a supportive person that you can trust.

What to Do in a Toxic Friendship

If your friendship is toxic, or if you suspect that it might be, the best thing you can do is to put some space between you two. You might notice the signs that there's something wrong, but especially if this is a long friendship that was once healthy, you might be tempted to remain in it. This isn't good for you or for your friend.

Try gradually putting distance between you, starting with declining invites to hang out or answering messages less frequently. You can also talk to a trusted adult about what's going on in your friendship to get help if you need it.

Chapter 11: Managing a Group

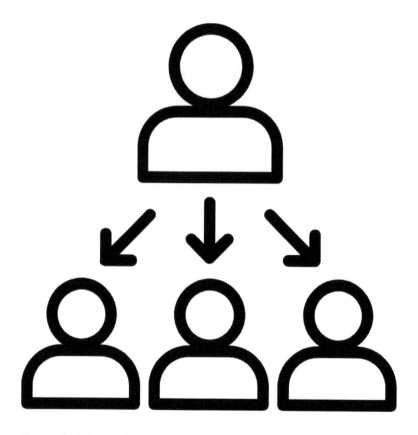

In adulthood, leadership is one of the most desirable traits for success. It's necessary in just about every job and can help you to work better in a group setting. Even if you never intend to be a leader in your adult life, having the skills to lead and manage a group will serve you well.

This skill helps you to inspire others, to achieve goals, and to connect with those around you.

For some people, leadership comes naturally. For others, it can be difficult to foster. The good news is that you can learn how to be a good team player and how to be a good leader. School often sets the foundation for this with group projects where you and a handful of other students have to come together to create something to share with the class. Sports can also help foster this sort of teamwork, especially if you find yourself in the position of leading your team.

If school and sports aren't your forte, consider this example: Being a good group manager can help you in video games if you're playing with a team. If you can step into that leadership role, you can make sure everyone's cooperating and working toward the same goal.

So, how do you learn how to manage a group and be a good leader? Here are a few tips:

Practice Communicating

The most important part of managing a group is being able to communicate clearly with everyone. After all, what's a leader who can't communicate well? The answer's simple: ineffective. You don't have to be the most talkative person in your group to be the leader either – you just have to be willing to listen, ask questions, and understand how everyone can work together to achieve your goals.

Admittedly, that's a lot to expect at your age, but remember, this is a life skill that's meant to come with practice and time! It's something that adults continue to practice regularly. All you have to do is set the foundation.

When you sit down in a group, make sure that you talk to each person when dividing up work or assigning tasks, and when you do, it should be tailored to individual strengths and weaknesses. This means that you'll probably have to ask everyone questions about what they're good at and what they struggle with, and then figure out how to organize this information.

Communication practice can come from outside of a group setting, too. You can, for example, work on communicating one-on-one with friends or when giving speeches in class. Remember that part of being a good communicator is having good body language, so you should be making eye contact when talking, smiling, and keeping your hands out of your pocket.

Work With Others Regularly

Another way to improve your ability to lead a group is to make sure that you practice working with others. The more you work in a group setting, the easier being in this environment gets for you. Collaboration is something that everyone should know how to do, especially because it's so essential in adulthood. Almost every job will require you to collaborate to some degree, even the ones that you might initially think would be solo jobs. You have to talk to customers and clients. Authors may work with editors and marketers.

If it's hard for you to work with others because you're shy, the best thing you can do is keep on practicing. Start out by working in groups that you can trust, like your friends. The more you do this, the easier it will become.

One way that you can get more experience with other people is in volunteer groups. These offer a great way for you to get out, get around new people, and work in a group setting to achieve a similar goal. It's one of my favorite options to suggest for tweens. Find something you're passionate about and see if there are any volunteer opportunities in your area. For example, maybe you love pets. See if you can volunteer at your local humane society or at a pet rescue near you. Not only will you get to enjoy the fuzzy companions, but you'll also be able to talk about your shared interests with other people.

Practice Organization

Have you ever been in a group for a project that was completely disorganized? I have, and let me tell you, it's tough. It's hard to create something cohesive when one person never shows up, one person never does any work, one person does the *wrong* work, and then all the pieces are lost because the leader forgot their binder on the school bus, and it's gone.

If you want to manage a group and be a good team leader, you need to be at least somewhat organized. Take notes when figuring out who will do what so that everyone is on the same page about details. Use planners to make sure that everyone has their work done on time. As you do this, you'll help the whole group function like it should and the whole team will come together easier and more effectively.

Work on Negotiation Skills

Not all groups are peaceful, and as the leader, that puts you in a pretty awkward position. People will turn to you to solve the problem or conflict, which can be tough if you don't know what you're doing. That's why you need negotiation skills. These help you to find a better solution to the problem by discussing what issues have arisen and what the people with the conflict want or need to resolve it.

Ultimately, the most important thing to remember when trying to negotiate a solution is that it should be win-win. Negotiations mean compromise so that everyone feels like they are heard and can work well together. For example, maybe you're doing a group report on how tornadoes form. Your group agrees that Allie will talk about thunder and lightning, Brad will talk about how tornadoes form, and Chris will provide information about some of the biggest tornadoes ever recorded.

Well, Chris shows up with information about how tornadoes form, and so does Brad. How can you negotiate the situation so neither person feels like they have to do double work? If your answer is that you'll gather the information about big tornadoes, you're wrong.

You need to be able to walk them through the problem. In this case, if you were organized, you'd have notes that Chris was supposed to provide the information about the biggest tornadoes. In this case, you might offer to let Brad use some of Chris's information in his part of the project so that Chris doesn't feel like he wasted his time, and ask if he can get the correct information.

He might not be happy, but by being able to pull out your notes to show that Chris was wrong, you were able to slow the conflict and find a solution that at least somewhat works for everyone.

Practice, Practice, Practice!

Finally, the last thing to remember is to practice! Leadership isn't easy for most people, so take every opportunity you can to foster it. Volunteer to take charge when opportunities arise. You may volunteer to help with your siblings at home, or to help your friends complete a project. There are so many opportunities available where you can work on those skills and really hone them. And before you know it, being a leader will start to come naturally to you!

Chapter 12: Developing a Serve-First Mindset

This chapter is a continuation of the previous one. In this chapter, we're going to start talking about developing a serve-first mindset, which is used in leadership to help leaders engage with their teams. It's also useful as a concept in just about every aspect of your life, especially if you're the kind of person who honors altruism. Altruism is like selflessness. It's the desire to do good things for other people out of a genuine and selfless concern for their wellbeing. In other words, it's choosing to do things to help others that have no benefit to you simply out of the goodness of your heart. It might sound like a silly thing to do. After all, there should always be something in it for you, right?

Nope!

It's great to take a selfless approach, as long as you balance it with self-respect and care for yourself. Altruism is one of those values that some people just have. They want to make sure that the people around them are taken care of and feel good, and they'll do whatever it takes to help others, within reason.

Let's talk about Kayla for a minute. Kayla is 12, like you. She's smart, funny, and kind. One of her favorite things to do is help people around her and watch the ripple effect. She likes to hide painted rocks with kind messages on them, she volunteers at the local retirement home to spend time with seniors, and at home, she's always quick to ask if her parents need any help. It makes her feel good to help others, and other people notice this about her.

At school, Kayla is well-liked because people know that they can rely on her to help when they need it. They know that she'll always do her fair share in group assignments, and she's quick to help people around her if they drop something.

The truth, though, is that Kayla has a hard time saying "no" when someone needs something from her. She has a hard time telling herself that she doesn't have to volunteer for something when a teacher asks for help when she's tired. She has a hard time finding the line between selflessness and losing self-respect.

This is hard even for adults. Knowing where to draw that line can be tough because it's hard to know when altruism and selflessness are harmful to you. If you're like Kayla and find yourself so focused on what you can do for others and not on what you can do for yourself, you're not alone, but you do need to learn how to find that line.

Altruism and Leadership

Altruism can take a lot of different forms. For example, maybe you give up your seat on the bus to an elderly person so they can sit down, and you choose to stand for the rest of the ride, instead. Standing up didn't benefit you at all, but it did benefit the senior who needed to sit to ride the bus safely.

Another example can be choosing to surprise your parents by making dinner because they're sick and you want them to be able to rest. By cooking dinner, you benefit your parents at the cost of your own time, but you do it because you care about your parents.

Altruism has its own place in leadership, too. When you're a leader, you're responsible for everyone you oversee, and that means making sure that everyone's needs are met. You may need to juggle work, or take on a few parts of a project to help out because, ultimately, the success of your project depends on the success and wellness of your team.

In leadership, the "serve first" theory sees leaders behaving altruistically. As a result, the team feels more engaged and cared for, meaning they work harder in return. In the serve first theory, leaders should lead from a genuine desire to better serve the needs of others instead of leading because they want the authority that comes with the title.

By engaging the needs and wants of your team or group, you get more cooperation. You also get something even more important: loyalty. Now, in a group project, loyalty probably won't play much of a role, but when you get your first job, you'll learn that a little loyalty can go a long way.

The same can apply in your personal relationships. When you take on a serve-first mentality to your relationships, you honor the needs and wants of those around you (within reason). Of course, that doesn't mean that you should go out and only do what other people want from you. You still need to have self-respect and meet your own needs, but it's also important to have a genuine interest and to genuinely care for other people.

How to Be Altruistic

Being altruistic means that you're willing to behave selflessly for other people. As long as you act out of a genuine desire to help, altruism can be a fantastic thing. In fact, it can have a bunch of positive effects on you and your friendships. For example, being altruistic can help you to have a better sense of mental well-being. This is because when you do things for other people out of the kindness of your heart, you often feel good about yourself. Helping other people is typically associated with feelings of happiness, which can overall improve self-respect and self-worth.

If you want to be altruistic, there are some ways that you can begin changing your actions to encourage it. For example:

- **Seek Out Inspiration:** Do you know anyone who's particularly altruistic? Maybe you think of your parents – after all, raising a child is one of the most selfless things a person can do with all the care and attention that goes into it. Or, you could have a teacher who you know stays late each day to help students with homework who won't have help at home. See what other people are doing to improve the world and take a page out of their books. You might be surprised at some of the ways you come up with to help others!

- **Be Empathetic:** Altruism relies in part on empathy. Empathy allows us to put ourselves in the shoes of other people and experience their emotions like they were our own. For example, if you see someone crying at school, you might immediately feel bad for them and think about how you'd feel if you were in their shoes. That's a form of empathy. Empathy helps you to connect to those around you instead of distancing yourself. Empathy is an important social skill because it allows you to understand where people are coming from, which can help you to help them.

- **Set a Goal to Help:** Another way to practice altruism is to try to make it a habit. You can do this by setting a goal that every day that you'll try to help at least one person. One random act of kindness each day can be enough for you to really connect with people around you and get into the habit of being caring toward everyone, regardless of whether you'll benefit. You can volunteer, hold open doors in public, help a friend or family member with a chore, or come up with other ways to help. Over time, you'll make kindness a habit.

A Warning About Altruism, Serving, and Self-Respect

Of course, kind acts and altruism are only kind and good if they aren't done at your expense. It's okay for you to not benefit from something you've chosen to do, but you don't want your kindness to become harmful to you. It can be a difficult line to avoid crossing when choosing an altruistic, serve-first perspective for life. Altruistic acts shouldn't put you in danger or set you back significantly. You don't have to do everything that people ask of you to be altruistic. In fact, doing so is a great way for you to burn out, which isn't going to help anyone.

You still need to balance your own boundaries and self-respect when choosing to behave altruistically. This means recognizing that your own values and how you care for yourself are still significant. You need to remember to engage in self-care and avoid giving too much of yourself to the people around you that you want to help. Choosing an altruistic approach to life can cause people to choose to neglect themselves to care for others, but the problem here is that it becomes unmanageable. It's not sustainable, just like we discussed earlier with the example about trying to pour from an empty cup.

A helpful way to look at this is that selfishness and selflessness exist on a spectrum, just like colors. You can have black and white and all the shades of gray in between. Likewise, you have selfishness and selflessness existing with all the shades between them. When you practice self-care, you're choosing to put yourself somewhere in the middle instead of being on one extreme or the other.

Selfishness is when you put your own needs first to the detriment of others. Selflessness is putting everyone else's needs above your own. Self-care is somewhere in the middle, where you respond to your own needs while still considering the impact that doing so will have on others.

It's not self-indulgent to keep your cup full with self-care; it lets you continue to be altruistic in the future. Self-indulgence can be selfish and involves doing things that you want in a way that will benefit you and help you to avoid a situation. Self-indulgence could be eating that big piece of chocolate cake because you're stressed about school, even though the cake isn't going to do anything other than temporarily make you feel better. Now, there's nothing wrong with chocolate cake, but it's also not a very effective or healthy way to cope with or manage stress.

Self-care is about taking care of yourself. It's about finding ways to motivate yourself toward change and growth over time. Self-care can include treating yourself just because you'd like a treat, but you're not relying on that treat to make you feel better. You're enjoying it for what it is, instead. Self-care is important because it helps you become resilient.

Conclusion

Hey, kids! You made it to the end of the book! There was so much for you to discover, from how to respect yourself to managing money and friendships. These life skills are here to help you live a happy, comfortable life, teaching you how to interact with others and how to get through difficult situations.

As you grow up, it's hard to keep up with the constant changes around you. People are growing and maturing. Your friends might start developing new interests that make it hard to spend time together. You might drift apart from people you've been close to for years, or you might notice that your friends are trying to take advantage of you and your kindness.

You might feel insecure or worried about your position in life, and that's understandable. You're maturing into an adult and that means that things aren't the same as they used to be. Your interactions with other people can become more complex. That's why we went through all the life skills we covered.

All of these begin with a champion mindset. Knowing that you can change and grow as a person is at the heart of nearly every skill we talked about. It can help you to stand up for yourself, even if you're shy, because you know that you can develop your skills and learn from your struggles and failures.

Remember, ultimately, you are in control of your life, especially as you get older. You get to make decisions about yourself and who you want to be. You get to choose your friends and choose when to walk away when something doesn't seem quite right. You have the power to be whatever you want in life if you put your mind to it.

And remember, when things get tough, there are trusted grownups in your life that you can rely on to help you. Remember to go back to that list of trusted adults you wrote down at the beginning of the book. Ask them for help when things get tough or if you find yourself in a position where you need an adult's perspective.

There's nothing wrong with relying on other people when you need guidance!

Now, get out there and put these skills to work!

Leave Your Feedback on Amazon

Please think about leaving some feedback via a review on Amazon. It may only take a moment, but it really does mean the world for small authors like myself :)

Even if you did not enjoy this title, please let me know the reason(s) in your review so that I may improve this title and serve you better.

From the Author

As a retired school teacher, my mission with this series is to create premium educational content for children that will help them be strong in the body, mind, and spirit via important life lessons and skills.

Without you, however, this would not be possible, so I sincerely thank you for your purchase and for supporting my life's mission.

Don't forget your free gifts!

(My way of saying thank you for your support)

Simply visit **haydenfoxmedia.com** to receive the following:

- 10 Powerful Dinner Conversations To Create Amazing Kids

- 10 Magical Affirmations To Help Kids Become Unstoppable in Life

(you can also scan this QR code)

More titles you're sure to love!

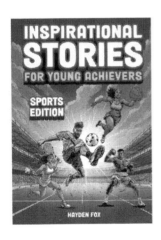

HAYDEN FOX

Made in the USA
Middletown, DE
17 October 2023

40833353R10080